THE GREATEST ADVENTURE OF ALL

a personal recollection of Romania

THE GREATEST ADVENTURE OF ALL

a personal recollection of Romania

by William R. Steinmetz

Copyright © 2020 by William R. Steinmetz
The Greatest Adventure of All
a personal recollection of Romania
by William R. Steinmetz
Printed in the United States of America

1st Edition
ISBN: 978-0-578-71079-2

All rights reserved. The author guarantees all contents are either original or are in public domain and do not infringe upon the legal rights of any other person or work. No part of this publication may be reproduced or transmitted in any form or by any means, electronic or mechanical, including photocopying, recording, or any information storage or retrieval system, without the permission in writing from the author.

All scripture quotations are taken from the the New King James Version of the Bible Copyright © 1982 by Thomas Nelson, Inc., Nashville, Tennessee, United States of America

www.granvilleassemblyofgod.com

THE GREATEST ADVENTURE OF ALL
a personal recollection of Romania

CONTENTS

DEDICATION..
FOREWORD...

1. It Started With a Nudge 1
2. A Winter Trip the Hard Way, Innocents Abroad 3
3. Enthusiasm Shared Goes Viral, Well Sort of 9
4. The Big Trip "Hey, What Could Go Wrong?" 15
5. Trips Continue *and* Flying is Allowed 35
6. It's Hard to Help; It really Is..39
7. More on the Beginning: How It All Began 43
8. The Lord Blessed with RTSC *and* Our Love for the Romanian People Deepened 47
9. A Call to a Greater Commitment..................................53
10. Settling in to Roman *and* Those Wonderful Orphan Teenagers..57
11. Bacau Beckons ... Then Fades to Another Call 63
12. A Call to Humble Service (Granville AG) *and* an Unfinished Story...67

EPILOGUE...69
IN CLOSING...93

DEDICATION

One can't describe a great adventure without recognizing the key figures who made the adventure possible. While it might sound trite to some, my number one person to recognize is Jesus Christ. I have a personal relationship with Him, and I try to walk with Him every day. He rescued me from an awful fate and set my feet on a path you'll read about. He is my Lord, my Savior, and my friend.

My second recognition is my wife, Judy. She is my soul mate, my BFF, my partner in marriage for more than 49 years now, and the one person who has made all my journeys, including this great adventure, not just possible but a joy. She didn't join me on all of these journeys to Romania, but when she did, our friends there noticed a difference in me. "Bill is more happy when Judy travels with him," they would often say. True, during this great adventure … and true, for all of the 49 plus years we have been together.

A thank you also to our many Romanian friends who you will read about in this book, including Cos, Alina, George, Mugur, Anca, Valerica, Ana M., Marian, and Estera. Your love, hospitality, encouragement, and joy in the Lord made this adventure a pleasure.

Finally, a special thank you to Pamela Bolton. Pamela has toiled long hours on this book, turning an engineer's version of English into a readable story. More importantly, God sent her along at just the right time to encourage me to finish. "Exceptional," this daughter of encouragement said. It remains for you to read, digest, and consider.

FOREWORD

DR. DUANE DURST
Network Superintendent
New York Ministry Network, Assemblies of God

The question may be asked, "Where have you been?" But better to ask how one got there and the lessons learned along the way. In "The Greatest Adventure of All" the better questions are answered; the stories of lessons learned and the miracles along the way will encourage the reader on their own journey not just to get there but to enjoy the trip! Bill and Judy's "Great Adventure" built faith, experience, and wisdom, which I have been blessed to be on the receiving end of Bill's counsel and insight. Their adventure continues as the Steinmetzes lead multiple New York congregations from their home in Vermont.

REVEREND PATRICK HILKEY
Senior Pastor
Evangel Assembly of God, Buffalo, New York

This book is all about adventure! When I first met Bill in 1993, in Granville, NY, I did not think of him as an adventurous person. But after hearing about his early stories in Romania and then joining him in several adventures myself, I found that he is one of the most adventurous people I know. Romania grew on me as I ventured into that part of the world, and I have truly been changed by being part of Bill's adventure. Please join the adventure, and enjoy the read, because it will be worth your time. Following Christ is all about adventure and worth the journey! Who knows? Maybe you will be on an adventure yourself someday. Enjoy this one for your faith to grow.

EUROPE

ROMANIA

Chapter 1

It Started With a Nudge

"In the beginning
God created the heavens and the earth."
Genesis 1:1

It really did! It started with a nudge in the ribs, from God by the way. I was a recently unemployed management consultant starting my own practice from my home in the south of England. How my family got there from our home in Pennsylvania is a story in itself. But suffice it is to say, I had gone from a hyper-busy lifestyle to one with lots of extra time, as I searched out my first clients.

So, there I was watching the BBC on a midmorning, where a month ago I was administering the London office of Booz Allen & Hamilton, while attending to my own clients in the transportation field. As I said, I had been hyper busy. I was now hyper "not" busy. Quite a difference, yet God can use those humbling, seemingly unimportant times for extraordinary purposes.

So the nudge came, while I was watching the BBC's report on Romania. It was 1991, the iron curtain was down, and some of the terrible excesses of communism were being exposed. Some of the worst were in Romania where the dictator, Ceaucescu, had required women to have a minimum of five children to build a "great" nation. In many cases, families could not afford this in a badly broken economy; and the extra children were placed in State orphanages. The BBC was exposing how bad conditions were for tens of thousands of children. Heartbreaking!

And there it was ... the nudge. I heard a voice say to me: "You can go!" You can go??? Now, I had a family to look after, two daughters rapidly approaching college age and a wonderful wife who I had encouraged to retire from teaching when times were good. I had no income. I can go??? It made no practical sense, and I wrestled with my very western response to need — we can send some money. But God kept nudging me with — "You can go!"

I did what I had been taught to do; I prayed on it. God kept nudging, "You can go!" So I started talking about the nudge with my wife, my Christian friends, and my pastor. To my amazement, they all thought it was a great idea and undoubtedly from God. I was less sure and prayed for confirmation. A dangerous prayer ... for in short order, God had provided a truck, materials to distribute when there (Romania needed everything), and very importantly, a little black book with lists of Christian contacts throughout Romania. The latter came from two ladies from our church, Margaret and Avril. They had a ministry of going into Romania in the communist days and "losing" Bibles to interested Romanians. Losing them was the only way back then, as distributing Bibles was forbidden.

So along with a map, some travel funds, and the required paperwork, I was set to go. The only problem was that I needed a codriver. It would take three days of driving with little sleep and lots of onerous border crossings to get there. This was no one-man trip. No one seemed to be available, and it seemed like I had an out. Then God provided the perfect codriver. Ronnie was my manager of administration from the London office, a former Sergeant Major in the Scots Guards, and a thoroughly capable guy. He was only missing one prerequisite – he wasn't a Christian, and this was a Christian trip. God had an amazing work planned. Ronnie thought he was just helping out his former boss, but God had a wonderful gift for him ... a gift that would change his life.

CHAPTER 2

A Winter Trip the Hard Way, Innocents Abroad

"Go therefore and make disciples of all the nations"
Matthew 28:19

It was February 1991, and every sensible resident of Britain was taking a winter break somewhere warm. British folks crave the sun, as winter's grey skies can wear you out. Back then, brochures from travel agents were everywhere right after Christmas, and February was peak "fly to the sun" time. Not so for Ronnie and me as we prepared to drive across Europe, across the Transylvania Mountains to some of the least accessible and least assisted parts of Romania – a 2,500 mile trip, one way. That was the plan, and with a great prayer team backing us up, off we went.

The first step was to drive the 7 ½-ton truck to a ferry terminal and cross the English Channel. Not very hard with the right paperwork and cash, and Ronnie and I took on the role of real truckers. Back then, the ferry companies were competing for the truck traffic, so us "real" truckers were offered a free breakfast in the truckers lounge. Actually, it was very pleasant until I shocked Ronnie by mixing my cereals together in one bowl. This seemed outrageous to him, but once he tried it, he found it quite pleasant. Oh, these Brits have so much to learn from us colonials!

The trip across western Europe (the EC) was tedious in 1991. Every country's border had a customs and immigration control with paperwork and delays. It was hard to drive just a few hours and see a long line of trucks at the next border crossing. We hadn't weighed the truck, and the 7 ½-ton limit was strictly enforced in places like Germany. But we plodded on from France, to Germany, to Austria, to Hungary, and finally to the border with Romania, which was not open at night. Ronnie and I had not slept for two days except for an occasional doze in the passenger seat, so the rest stop on the border of Hungary and Romania was a welcome stop.

We pulled up to a local truck stop and weighed up the virtue of food versus sleep. We were as hungry as we were tired but found the Hungarian menu indecipherable. The one item we could understand was "spiegle ei." My limited German translated that as "egg play." We ordered two, much to the amusement of our waiter. When they arrived, we realized why as each "spiegle ei" was a platter of six eggs with a small mountain of fried ham. We had no problem eating six eggs each, as we had not eaten a real meal since the ferry crossing two days earlier. After a short nap in the cab, viable only for the super tired, the border opened; and after the usual paper work nonsense, we were waved into the country of Romania.

My first images of Romania were quite ordinary. It was quite early, and there were few people about. The city of Oradea was fairly close to the border, so we pulled into the city while noticing some long stares from pedestrians. Many folks were walking, but we would later learn that few cars were rolling about at that hour or at any hour. Our contact in Oradea was an English couple whose mother went to our church in England. They were in the process of adopting a Romanian infant, and the bureaucracy was taking weeks. They were most gracious hosts and let us sleep in their apartment's living room. We shared the gifts sent from their family and our church, and we had a family party with them that night.

The next morning we started our serious mission work … well, giving stuff away to people who were doing real mission work. Our first mission contact was a lady named

Angela. She was an angel both in looks and service. She was running an outreach to orphanage children in Oradea, and we gifted her with some of the clothes, food, and medicines we had brought in. In the evening, we had a worship service together, and I remember praying in a circle with the children, Angela, and Ronnie.

That night as we prepared for bed, Ronnie asked me about the peace and joy he had experienced while we were praying. I explained that was the presence of the Holy Spirit, and about giving his heart to Jesus and how to be born again by praying a prayer of repentance. He took all that in very quietly, and I wondered whether my words had helped him. Well, the next morning he was so happy, I would describe him as giddy. I asked him what had changed and whether he had prayed the prayer of repentance to Jesus. He confirmed that he had, and the rest of the trip was more of a joy for him, as he was more fully aware of why we were making this trip — not just to help people practically but to encourage them spiritually to enter into an eternal relationship with Jesus. We were now Christian partners doing God's work joyfully. What a wonderful gift it is to serve God wholeheartedly, knowing that the only reason you are doing something is for the glory of God. And that is what this trip and future trips to Romania were all about.

From Oradea, we drove east across the Transylvania Mountains toward the northeast Moldavian region of Romania. We had chosen the northeast as we were told that was where the greatest need for aid was. That turned out to be correct, but what we didn't know was how difficult and dangerous crossing those mountains to get to Moldavia would be. We weren't much past Oradea when we began to climb higher and higher. It was night when we got to the most challenging part, and it seemed like there were endless switchbacks on snow covered roads. Being brothers in Christ, we prayed hard together as we edged our way around each tight corner, while fearing the deadly slide that braking too hard would cause. It was an advantage driving at night, as we later saw drop-offs at those many switchbacks that might have affected our nerves. Looking back, we are convinced that our prayers brought many angels to protect us.

We arrived in the middle of the night in Roman with nothing but a street address to guide us. We couldn't find it, and the local police only wanted to steal my flashlight. We finally asked for help from a man who was standing outdoors in the bitter cold. He looked like he was on a stakeout, and he might well have been. But he took pity on us and showed us around the back of the buildings where we could find people's names on mailboxes. We found the right apartment for George and went up and knocked on his door; it was something like 3 am. A trembling voice responded, and when we said we were from England, the door opened, and we were greeted with big smiles. All of George's family got out of bed to greet us and a party of sorts broke out. Anna started making an enormous breakfast, and we worked through simple translations to explain our mission. George was only too glad to help. He took off from work the next day and proceeded to introduce us to orphanages and others in need.

That first full night in Roman, we attended a service at the small Baptist church – a building no larger than a small house. We discovered that during the first night one of our tires had been slashed. This attracted great attention, and a good part of the town showed up to try to help. One of the lug nuts on the bad wheel was frozen on, so an arc welder was produced to get it off. They were about to proceed when one of the men pointed out they had not grounded the electric cutting torch to the truck. If they had proceeded without that, they would have fried the electronics on the truck. The truck might still be there today. Having observed that chaos, I went into the little church while allowing Ronnie to observe the rest. It was cold outside but very warm due to a wood fire inside, and the glasses I wore at that time instantly fogged up. I stumbled to a seat and gratefully sat down. Suddenly, George was pulling at my arm, "please, Bill, please." I thought that he just had another seat for me, but actually, it was to avoid embarrassment as I had taken a seat on the left side of the church, which was reserved for the women of the church – a real no-no in their culture. I would also learn that a Christian hug from me was for the men only and not the ladies. No hug, no matter how careful, was allowed between the genders, particularly in church. This was a real change from the church culture that we were used to in the US and Britain.

The next morning, we visited our first orphanage, and it was a shock. Hundreds of children were crammed into poor, often crumbling facilities with little to offer them. All of our gifts were greatly appreciated, and we felt honored to offer contributions of medications, clothing, and food to these sad operations. At one orphanage, our gift of light bulbs was most appreciated, as they had none. As we moved from room to room, the staff would screw a lightbulb in to illuminate dozens of children sitting/lying in bed in the dark. Then, they would unscrew the lightbulb and move on to another room where the illumination sequence would repeat itself. As we looked at these young, innocent faces and later received their hugs, we knew we were hooked and would do more to help them.

One of our saddest experiences was entering a room full of baby cribs with two children per crib. The administrator announced to us that all of these children would shortly die. When we asked how this could be, she told us that all of these children had AIDS. Russian "experts" had advised the Romanians that all babies should be given blood transfusions, and all of these children had been given the AIDS virus in that blood. They did, indeed, all die. The big government experts had ruined much of Romania, and these children had to pay a huge price for this particular folly. There would be more to come….

8

CHAPTER 3

Enthusiasm Shared Goes Viral, Well Sort of

"But you shall receive power when the Holy Spirit has comes upon you"
Acts 1:8

I remember driving the truck home after the three-day return trip and finding no one at home. I was so anxious to share my adventures with my family, and I was profoundly disappointed that I had to wait several hours to see them. But the wait was worth it, as my wife and two daughters hugged me and listened patiently to all my tales. These sweet hours of reunion were followed by other less pleasant emotions that I can best describe as disorientation.

I felt most disoriented when I went to our local supermarket. Now, to my American friends, I have to explain that a supermarket in England in 1991 was not what most of us are used to. The supermarket of that era in England was hardly super in size and not very super in variety. But to a returnee from eastern Europe, that supermarket was a parody of suburban glut. I remember staring at the almost endless supply of cereals. The last "supermarket" I had visited in Romania only had mineral water and pickled vegetables. We had looked out one night and saw a line of folks waiting in the cold for something in a dark alley. In the morning, I asked what that was all about and was advised that those were parents of babies hoping to buy some milk. The prices were low, but the supply was lower; and farmers had little incentive to sell their products in the cities. I would learn later that families survived by bartering and sharing. Big families with farms in the country did okay. Older, isolated folks were doing poorly; and the orphans ... well, we already knew about their sorry state.

My disorientation in a culture that I had been comfortable in just a few weeks before continued in work, social, and even church life. How was it all right that we had so much and they had so little? As I began to explain these feelings, I am sure many rolled their eyes or just felt uncomfortable. But some understood, and perhaps the simple video I had made of our trip helped them understand. I knew one thing — I had to go back. The bigger questions of how, why, and for what purpose still needed to be answered, but I knew that I had to go back.

Starting with my family, then with my church, and even with the folks at my former employer, I began to gather a circle of friends who wanted to help. The help they provided came in many forms — financial, encouragement, and gifts. But the most important help was those people who understood the urgency of the need and also wanted to go. Nowhere did that urgency resonate more than in our local church, Esher Green Baptist Church.

Now, at this point, I have to explain how a former acolyte from the Lutheran Church in America ended up as an Assistant Pastor of a Baptist church, and not just any Baptist church but a Penta-Baptist, Bapticostal, Holy Spirit-filled church. The year was 1987, and I was a brand-new partner at Booz Allen, flying all over Europe and making more money than I ever thought possible. I was in Milan for some business meetings and was scheduled for an early morning flight from Milan back to London for internal meetings at my office. I checked in for my flight and sat down in the gate waiting area. Then it happened. I can best explain it by what I now know it was — the power of God's Holy Spirit came upon me. Physically, I was bent over in my seat, and I don't believe I could have sat up if I had tried. I later described it as being like the thumb of God was holding me down. Emotionally I was in ecstasy, crying and praying all at the same time. My prayer was a simple, "Thank you Lord!" Unknown to me at this time, the ladies of the church were praying for the men of the church to receive the Holy Spirit at that very hour. I had been praying for years, a simple prayer: "Lord use my life!" Now, God ministered to me, at an airport of all places. I was to "live simply, help other people, and witness." He told me to give up alcohol and smoking. On the latter, He asked me, "Why would you pollute the temple of the Lord?" I was told to avoid ego in ministry, and then He sent me on my way. The man next to me on the plane got quite an earful about God, and I couldn't wait to tell Judy. But this kind of experience often causes controversy....

I couldn't wait to tell my pastor about my experience. To my surprise, Pastor Norman would not let me share this story with our church. When I asked him why, he explained that he had had a member in a previous church who believed they had an experience of God, but it turned out they were mentally unstable, so "no," I would not be permitted to share. This discussion shook me up, and Judy suggested that I speak with another pastor, David, who had recently baptized several of our teenaged friends. David explained that I had been baptized in the Spirit, that it was wonderful, and that I should be baptized in water as an adult believer, which I later did. I subsequently learned that my previous church, a Reformed church, was Calvinistic and did not believe in the baptism in the Holy Spirit at all.

A quick note about my water baptism in that little chapel in Esher, Surrey, England: It was a joyous experience, and as I prepared to go under the water, a member read from Isaiah 61: "The Spirit of the Sovereign Lord is on me, because He has anointed me to proclaim good news...." This was the text Jesus used in Nazareth to begin His ministry (Luke 4), and I was more than a little bit humbled. Who me? I would later learn that this anointing and calling is for all believers.

One more quick comment about that little Baptist chapel in Esher: It was at the altar of that chapel that I had the privilege of leading my Dad to the Lord. He had been an active Mason up to that time and had filled his head with all kinds of useless rituals. He admitted that he didn't know how to pray. But that night, he prayed to receive Jesus into his heart, and I believe that one day I will see him again in Heaven.

So, it was to this "not so Baptist," Baptist church that I brought a message. They had supported my first journey to Romania and rallied around me for subsequent trips and an ever-widening ministry.

Trip two was special, as Judy joined me, along with several folks from our church. This journey included another 7 ½-ton truck, but it also included our already venerable Toyota Hi-Ace van — affectionately nicknamed Moby, as it seemed quite large on most English streets. After much paperwork preparation (again!), we departed with a truck full of materials for the churches and orphanages and a van with expectant adventurers.

The folks with us on this trip included a retired English policeman (aka a "Bobby") and his wife. His wife said on the way there that the one thing she could not handle was seeing a horse mistreated. I had never seen that in Romania, yet within hours of entering the country, we saw a farmer whipping a foundering horse. Nearly hysterical over this incident, we all tried to calm her. Later on, I would remind her that she would see mistreatment of children, something much more egregious; yet, we would have to control our emotions.

Another person on this trip was a young lady, Jenny, who was full of energy and joy. She was our go-to person when we needed to find something in the back of our truck. She would boldly dive into the back of the truck and literally swim through the piles of clothing and bags to find just the right item for each location. What a blessing to have a team member with that energy and enthusiasm. It was on this trip that we learned one of our biggest faith lessons.

Buying fuel for our vehicles was always a key chore and expense for each trip. We quickly learned that fuel (diesel and gasoline) was much cheaper if we purchased them in Romania. So, on this second trip, we delayed purchasing fuel until we were in the country. To our dismay, we found that all the gas stations were out of fuel. At that time (still 1991), all gas stations (the company name was PECO) were owned by the Romania state; and the State had decided to drop supplies, or they just messed up. So we made it part way into the country to a small town we didn't know. We were very low on diesel fuel for our truck; and we were still a long way from our destination in northeast Romania. Fortunately, we had the little black book with us, and there was one name in the book for this town. So we called and asked if we could spend the night. Our key phrase was: "We are Christians from England." To our amazement, that was all the introduction we needed. We were directed to a warm apartment, fed a wonderful hot meal, and allowed to sleep on the sofa, chairs, and floor for the night. We awoke refreshed, but we still had a big problem.

The next day we were well fed and rested but no closer to solving our fuel problems. Our host said that he had a possible solution, while saying that Romania was a land of opportunities. He then advised us to go out to the road and hold out an empty canister as trucks drove buy. So we asked our ladies to pray for us as we fellows went out on the road, by our now stranded truck, and started waving our empty fuel canister at passing trucks. To our amazement, one after another, they stopped; and each siphoned out a liter or two of fuel for a payment. I am quite sure that this payment did not go back to their employer in most cases, but bless them anyway for stopping and helping us. So after collecting enough fuel to finish our trip to Roman, we could have stopped this begging process, but in my mind I thought: "Why not collect a little extra, as insurance?" But from that moment on, trucks would not stop.

A voice from inside said to me: "My grace is sufficient for you. Go!" So we left and made it safely onward ... well, not quite.

We continued eastward over the mountains until we passed through a town with an open PECO station. So we stopped for diesel fuel. We shouldn't have! Within just a few miles, our truck stopped running; and we found that our fuel filters were clogged with dirt. Fortunately, we were then close to Suceava, and a call to our friends there brought out a truck with fresh fuel and clean filters. I still remember dumping all that diesel fuel on the road in front of some farmers' homes. We didn't apologize, but we should have. Environmental priorities would have to wait, as hungry and sick orphan children were waiting. These are priorities that I still believe in.

I mention Suceava and the folks at the Baptist Church there who were very kind to us, and I hope we helped them in some small way. One of my sweetest memories is meeting Cristina from the Baptist Church during our first visit to Romania. She ran into town and guided us to her church to meet her uncle, Pastor Dan. Her energy and enthusiasm was one of the keys to our continued support in Suceava. It didn't surprise us to learn that several years later she married an American and moved to the States. I haven't seen her since; I wish her well and thank her for all her help in those early years.

CHAPTER 4

The Big Trip, "Hey, What Could Go Wrong?"

*"These things I have spoken to you,
that in Me you may have peace.
In this world you will have tribulation."*
John 16:33

Upon returning home from that trip, both Judy and I were committed supporters of the Romanian Renaissance. There was a particular label placed on us and other Christians so committed. We were called "Romaniacs." Our enthusiasm was brought back to our church, and that enthusiasm was contagious. This was putting our faith into action, and who could refuse to help those cute Romanian orphans? So, now we were experts. We knew how to do this. So, why not do a bigger trip with more people from our church? And why not bring a music team to do Christian concerts and lead worship in the churches we now knew? Why not do something bigger? "Hey, What could go wrong?" Plenty!

We approached a bus/coach company to provide a coach and drivers to take our team across Europe and into Romania. Our plan was to take this coach with its professional drivers, and some of our team from the church would take turns driving the 7 ½-ton truck that we had again leased. After much preparation, we left from our church after Sunday services with many prayers and good wishes. We were off for the south coast of England, for a ferry ride across the channel, and for the long drive across western Europe. It would be easy this time, as we had experience in making this trip; and we had professional drivers driving the coach. Easy, right? Not quite!

I took turns sleeping on the coach and driving our truck. After a long stint of driving across France and into Germany, I retired to the coach for a nap. I probably napped no more than an hour or so and awoke to check out our progress. I casually read one of those big blue signs they have all over Europe as we drove by and noted we were making really good progress toward Switzerland. Switzerland?! That's south, we needed to be headed east toward Austria and Hungary. I remember hustling forward to talk to our two professional drivers. I asked them what route they had chosen. They explained they had taken skiers this way on previous trips. I reminded them that we were not going skiing and that Eastern Europe was indeed to the east. They eventually conceded that point and turned the coach around. A few hours were lost, but hey, we now had the coach headed in the right direction with the truck following. So, we had our one glitch for this mission. Right? Not exactly!

We made it safely and smoothly through Austria and Hungary, and despite the lost hours, we made it early enough to the Romanian border to pass in that evening. All seemed to be going along so well, and we were all excited. The inevitable paperwork process began, and we had a big problem. Although I had remembered to obtain all the necessary visas and truck papers for the whole trip, I had somehow forgotten to get the letter of invitation from the Romanian embassy to bring our truckload of gifts to the orphanages. The border guards wanted to help us, but without the letter, the truck could not enter. No letter, no passage! Their advice was to drive back to Budapest, visit the Romanian embassy there, and obtain a letter of invitation from them. Would they provide it? Would they even speak enough English to understand our request? Hungarian is still a total mystery to me, and my Romanian at that time was not enough to order a cup of coffee. What to do? What could we do?

The coach could go in alone; the truck was not allowed entry. We were reluctant to split up the team. Budapest was a four-hour drive back west with no guarantee that we would get the coveted letter of invitation. Finally, one of the guards suggested we try at the same border again the next morning. The big bosses would be in their offices in Bucharest, and perhaps they would take pity on us. So we slept in the coach on the border, within a hundred yards of our destination. We slept, but we were fitfully unsure of what the new day would bring.

In the morning, a new set of border guards came on duty. New guards, but the same answer, "No entry!" We finally got them to call their bosses, but we got the same answer, "No entry!" Finally, we got the lead guard to review what we had in the truck. We opened the back of the truck, and all one could see was music equipment — amplifiers, keyboards, drum kits, and lighting equipment. You name it, we had it – all in the back of the truck, as that was loaded last. At the time, I was annoyed at our worship leader, Mark, for bringing all this equipment. I wondered if it would fit, and if not, what we could leave behind. I was annoyed, but I was wrong, because God, as always, had a plan. Our lead border guard looked at all this equipment that would return home to England and hence did not require a letter of invitation. He started to waiver. I remember our one coach driver encouraging him to change his mind. And it worked! Another phone call to the big bosses in Bucharest, and we were allowed entry. Our problems were solved! Well, not all of them....

We drove promptly through Oradea and headed eastward through the industrial area. We were elated, probably giddy, and looked forward to all that God was going to do. And then it happened ... all of sudden, a huge crash that continued, and looking at my rearview mirror, all I could see were giant barrels bouncing all over the road. We had been run into by a tractor hauling a long line of wagons with large metal barrels on them; thankfully, they were empty barrels. The damage to the truck was minimal, but then began the long, painful wait for the local police to show up. It was really a long wait, well at least over an hour. I paced back and forth next to the bus with my fellow travelers looking down at me. I felt six inches tall. It didn't matter that the accident was not my fault. The damage was done, and another long wait resulted just a few miles from our first delay.

Then I heard it, a clear whisper of a voice telling me: "You can run!" Seriously? Where to? Still the voice persisted: "You can run; run away!" In my humiliation, it at least seemed like an option. Of course, the voice was nonsense English. I have since learned that one of Satan's favorite temptations to us is to run away. In our culture today, running away has become wide-spread. Running away from marriages, running away from the responsibility of raising children, running away from reality, through drugs and alcohol …. Running away is a national epidemic, and Satan is behind much, if not all of it. I am glad that I did not run away on that day on the outskirts of Oradea. I am glad, and I learned a lot about humility and taking your medicine when things don't go so well.

Over the mountains we went, and we arrived at Roman, Suceava, and Iasi for church services and outdoor concerts. The most notable were in Iasi. Then, we learned that local police were not always pleased to allow these outdoor concerts. Our host pastors explained that the old ways died hard, that the Communist State Government was against any gathering they couldn't control, especially Christian gatherings. We couldn't get permission in Iasi (a bigger city on the very northeastern border with Moldavia and the Ukraine). We decided to try anyway and used our generator to power our keyboard and sound system. Then, we noticed smoke coming from the keyboard, and we hurriedly unplugged the system, but the damage was done. I'm no electronics engineer, but I do know that smoke from electronics is a bad sign. So, what could we do? We prayed over the keyboard, laid hands on it claiming healing in the name of Jesus, and then tried again. Much to our amazement, everything worked beautifully.

In the evening, the Baptist Church in Iasi allowed us to perform a concert in their front yard. It was beautiful as the church property was surrounded on three sides by apartment buildings. Upon hearing our Christian music, folks opened their windows, looked out, and went out on their small patios to listen. It was like playing a concert in a grotto surrounded by eight-story-high bleachers. The applause and encouragement after each song was wonderful. God moved beautifully that night. Something very beautiful personally happened that night also.

Our youngest daughter had come on this trip under duress. She had heard about our earlier adventures and admitted she was sick and tired of hearing us talk about Romania. We encouraged her to come along, and she finally agreed, stating that she'd come along if it would shut down all the talk about Romania.

Well, that magical evening in Iasi, with temperatures just right and Christian music hanging in the air, our daughter had a God appointment. It came in the person of a teenage girl and her family. They met and got to know one another. She visited their home and learned what their simple life was like in the then bankrupt Romanian economy. They encouraged her and our entire team in what we were doing. Our daughter's heart was truly touched by their witness, and I can tell you that she has never been the same again. Rebellion was replaced by faith. It has grown for her into a deep faith in God, resulting in a wonderful family and a full-time Christian ministry helping young mothers with parenting. God is so good! Years later, when Romanians would thank me for coming to their country and helping, I would often say, "No ... Thank you! Romania helped give me back my daughter. I will be forever grateful to Romania."

It was during this series of trips that we saw a number of healing miracles take place, and that increased our faith. On one walk over to the orphanage in Roman, one of our team members stepped into one of Roman's many potholes and dislocated her ankle; I mean dislocated it at a weird angle. After prayer and some gentle massaging, that ankle popped right back in place; and she was walking again, carefully but walking. On another occasion, we offered prayer for healing; and a lady with a shriveled hand came forward and was prayed for. We had moved on and were praying for others when we heard a shriek. The lady with the previously shriveled hand came running up waving her perfectly formed hand. God is so good!

All Gifts Welcome

In the early days, Romania needed everything from lightbulbs, to toilet paper, to food and medicines. We found that empty Coke cans were particularly treasured by young people who decorated their rooms with them. We were always happy to oblige.

Truck Driving

The basic skills came naturally to me, although maneuvering in tight places did cause me some trouble and some scrapes on several occasions. Ronnie W. had trained soldiers to drive trucks in the British Army, so I had the ideal co-driver. He said my driving was "smooth" on one occasion; I took that as a compliment.

Truck Loading for Early Trip

Through the Transylvania Mountain Foothills

"Romaniac" Defined

One who feels a call to help a people in the faraway land of Romania who through no fault of his or her own fell into terrible privation. Most severe cases were those people called by God. The illness was without cure.

Transylvania Mountain Village

One of Many Farmer Horse Carts

Church Culture

The churches in Romania that we worked with had been locked down by the Communist government for decades. Essentially illegal, local police would ignore them if they stayed in their small house locations with little or no signing. As a result, their culture and songs were definitely from the 1950's and earlier, which was fine. But some of the dress and social norms were a bit extreme.

Orphanage Kids Slept Two to a Crib

Pentecostal House Church During Communist Era

Early Poignant Moment

Seeing children in the countryside waving and begging for candy as we drove by rural villages. We obliged, of course, by throwing out hard candy.

Bibles as Gifts

Nearly everyone wanted one, but not just any Bible. They wanted a black Bible with a gold cross on it — an icon to be put on the shelf. We learned to give out New Testaments only, and on subsequent trips, those who evidenced reading the New Testament would receive their "icon" Bible.

Orphanage Kids – They Adopted You

Orphanage Kids – There Were Thousands

"Tata Bill" Reference

One bedridden lady was particularly enthusiastic during our visits and called me "Tata Bill" (Father Bill). We never learned her name, so we called her the Tata Bill lady. We learned quickly in nursing homes that we did not need to speak Romanian, nor really say anything. The people just wanted to have their hands held and to be listened to, which we gladly did, mostly in ignorance of what they were saying.

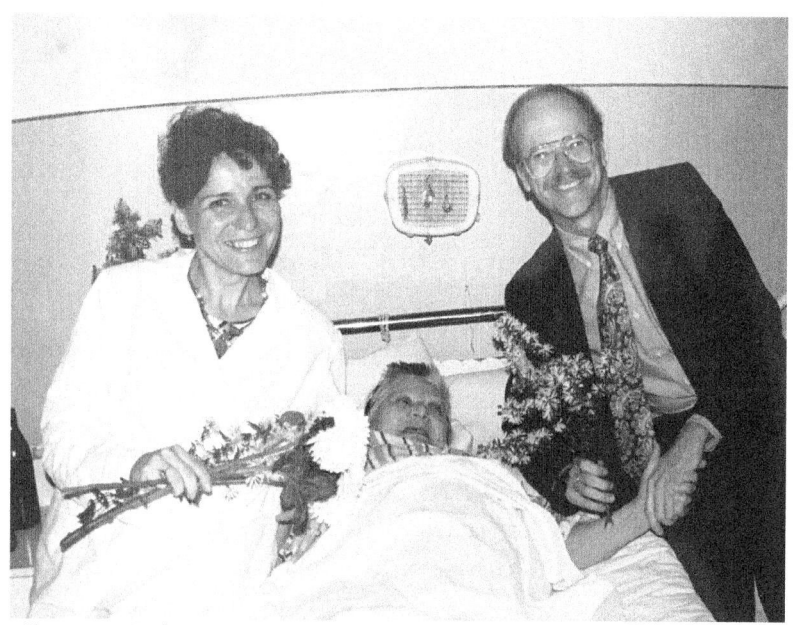

Doctor Director at Old Folks Home with "Tata Bill"

Suster Family, Roman, with Grandmother and Grandfather

"Mamaliga" Recipe

The dinner staple of most Romanians is really what we call corn pone. Simple to prepare but amazingly good when served with sour cream (semantena) and jalapeño peppers (arday utz). It is made by folding corn meal into boiling water until it becomes the right consistency. Garnish and eat quickly.

Wonderful Stuff!

Birthday Celebrations, Important Family Times

Sorin, George, and Ana with Judy and Me

CHAPTER 5

Trips Continue *and* Flying Is Allowed

***"Therefore we will not fear,
even though the earth be removed"*
Psalm 46:2**

By 1992, our local church had adopted Romania as a mission project. Over the next five years, a total of 60 members out of 200 would make at least one trip. There were different roles for these individuals, and as with any human endeavors, there was a core of people who did most of the work — the 80/20 rule. One key person to our efforts was Joan. At the time of the first Romania trips, Joan was going through a great deal of change in her personal life. The Romania mission work provided an important focus for her life at that time and helped her to grow in confidence that God loved her and would use her. She was much loved by the Romanian children, especially a youngster named Carmen. In fact, that tended to happen more and more as we continued to visit over the years. Individual orphan children would bond with an adult or couple, and of course, they would want to be adopted. For Judy and me, the young lady who most associated with us was Alina. She was a very sweet youngster with an eye defect that hurt her confidence. We had to decide early on if we were going to let our relationships with one or two children grow deeper or continue to work with many — there were about 60 youngsters that we began to focus upon helping in the one Roman orphanage. We decided not to adopt, and we would tell them we "adopted" all of them. This seemed to satisfy them, but

Alina continued to give long, soulful looks with her beautiful brown eyes.

We were making up to four trips a year at this point, and the products we had been trucking in were now generally available in Romania at competitive prices. So we looked into flying into Bucharest and driving north either with a rental car or by being picked up by one of our friends. Our first flying episode was with Air Tarom, the Romanian Airline; and the aircraft was a Russian Tupolev jet. The seats were aluminum frames with nylon webbing. It was clear this was a converted light bomber. Judy and I were accompanied by Joan on this first trip by airplane, and Joan was very nervous. We told her to concentrate on reading Scripture. I blurted out, "Pray over Psalm 46." She dove into the Word and found great comfort where it says, "God is our refuge and strength, an ever-present help in trouble. Therefore we will not fear, though the earth give way ... There is a river whose streams make glad the city of God, the holy place where the Most High dwells. God is within her, she will not fall; God will help her at break of day." We comforted ourselves with the knowledge that if the plane did go down, we were making this trip for God and Him alone. There certainly was no other reason to commute back and forth to Romania and especially to the remote northeastern, Moldavian region.

We were still working with several orphanages at this point, and we came upon the idea of helping several by hiring Christian workers at our own expense and providing them to the orphanages. We were able to set up the funding for this project and then went back to set up this program at several orphanages. Traveling with me for this purpose was Joan's daughter, Jenny, who had specific medical and administrative skills. We flew into Bucharest airport but arrived late, as the plane was delayed and the rental car company office was closed for the day. We were stuck in Bucharest for the night with no overnight accommodation options — hotels had a very bad reputation at this time. Then, we thought of the little black book our friends had given us, and we looked up a Bucharest person, called them, and asked if we could stay the night with them. The Christian network blessed us again when they said, "yes," and gave us directions to their home. The adventure didn't end there, for they assumed Jenny and I were husband and wife and fixed up one bed for us. After some embarrassing explanations in pigeon Romanian, we had two sleeping places provided. But their generosity will never be forgotten. The next day, after a hearty breakfast, we traveled back to the airport and rented our car for the trip north. We did complain to the staff about how they had left us stranded. This was not an unusual customer standard in Romania. At a personal level, the Romanians were warm and kindhearted. But in their official roles, they were often haughty and difficult. We would learn more about this other side of the Romanian personality on this trip.

Jenny and I had good success in Roman. The Roman orphanage agreed to accept our offer of the free help of 12 workers, and we were able to hire the ladies, who were mainly from churches we were working with in Roman. But in the town to the south, Falticeni, things did not go so well. They were at first quite interested and even excited to work with us. The Administrator called the headquarters and suddenly everything changed. A stone wall was raised and the answer was "No." We tried to understand why free help to improve the conditions for their children would be refused, but we never got a straight answer. My own theory was that a bureaucrat somewhere in government found it easy to say no, even if it hurt the children. The haughty and difficult side of the Romanian personality raised its ugly head. It wouldn't be the last time on this trip.

We left for the airport and our flight home. It was early morning and quite dark. Outside one town, we got stopped by a policeman in a white hat — indicating a traffic officer. He explained in broken English that we had crossed a white line somewhere, and we had to pay him money — bani! We knew from our friends that these were usually bribe payments, so I refused to pay. He made us follow him to the police station, and he ushered me into the station. I had Jenny stay outside the station and told her to pray hard. He said, "bani."

And I said, "No!" He made a point of showing me his not-very-nice jail cell with iron bars, and he asked again for money. By the way, there was no ticket provided for my offense, indicating all the bani would go to this particular policeman's pocket. When I said, "no," again, he asked me why I said no. I explained that we were in Romania to help the orphanage children, his children, and all the money I had would be used for them. He gave a long stare and then said, "plec" (or go). I was so pleased that I gave him a bearhug, as I had been doing to all the Romanian men in the churches. This clearly shocked him, but he still let me go. The communist system had taught the Romanians many bad habits, but a corrupt police force was one of the worst.

But the good news is that we successfully set up one orphanage project in Roman, and along with helping improve conditions for the children, we provided a small income for the twelve Christian ladies we employed. There would be problems and administrative headaches along the way, but at least we were able to help a little. The Romanian verb that means "to help" is "ajutor." As we used this word, we found it didn't mean help in the general sense; it meant money. When the cash didn't flow immediately, some Romanians were disappointed. We were learning that helping, truly helping others, is very hard work.

Chapter 6

It's Hard to Help; It Really Is!

*"So we may boldly say:
'The LORD is my helper; I will not fear.
What can man do to me?'"*
Hebrews 13:6

During this time, one of the leaders of the Baptist church in Roman, George, became a good friend and our local administrator. When I offered to pay him, he said, "no." He wanted to work like me, for free, for God's glory only. George was a great help in many ways, and I will always be grateful for his assistance. George's wife, Ana, was also very kind to us. On our first visit to Roman, Ana got up at our 3 am arrival and made Ronnie and me a very welcome meal. During later visits, Ana and George noticed that I particularly liked one type of salami; and after that, it was always on the menu. They spoiled me even though it was an expensive item for them. It was only years later that I learned that salami, named Sibiu salami, was specially made in a Romanian town named Sibiu and was made of horse meat. Well, it tasted good at the time.

Shortly after our third and fourth trips to Romania, I received an urgent notice from George that a single mom named Maria, in Roman, had been hit by a vehicle while crossing a street and needed special equipment for surgery. The equipment is called an external hip fixator and allows orthopedic surgeons to secure a broken hip for an extended period of time, while the hip bone knits together. We tried to get a supplier to donate one or at least offer a discounted price. My appeals fell on deaf ears, and the supplier of this gear in England had no interest in helping out. Several thousand dollars were sent off to get the fixator for Maria's surgery. We visited her in the hospital and prayed for her. Our hearts were broken as she pleaded for someone to look after her son. To my knowledge, we never were able to help her son; and sadly, Maria died shortly after our visit. This is one of a seemingly endless chain of tragedies set into motion by a heartless dictator and an extreme socialist economy.

One of the good things that resulted from trying to help Maria was that we got to know the staff at the local hospital. One of the surgeons asked if there was any way they could receive an air conditioner for their surgery theater. Apparently they were performing surgeries in the summer in extreme heat and humidity without the benefit of air conditioning. We took on the task and again quickly learned that the relevant corporations were unwilling to help — even a little. Nevertheless, we purchased a commercial air conditioning unit and shipped it to Heathrow Airport. Our administrator had an indication that British Airways would "pay the freight," but once there, BA staff disavowed any knowledge, so another big charge went on my beleaguered credit card. Anyway, the AC unit eventually showed up at Bucharest Airport. Unfortunately, the fun really began as airport staff said that special fees (code usually for a bribe) were needed to be paid. Again, George came to our rescue and met with the airport staff, and eventually the AC unit arrived in Roman. All of this led us to the conclusion that became a hallmark of our work in Romania — "It is not easy to help."

Our links to other churches helped us on many occasions. The AG church in Marcy, New York, near Utica, sent several teams to help. Later in our work, we had a close working relationship with one orphanage in Roman. This led to the great playground project on the orphanage grounds. I built a fence around the playground, while Pastor Pat (Pastor of the AG church in Marcy) performed more complex projects. During these visits from the church in Marcy, an older gentleman, Brother Dominick, made a big impact on the orphanage children. His gift was simply taking time to talk with the orphan kids. While the rest of us buzzed around building things, Dominick spent his time wisely – building relationships with the young orphans, encouraging them, and building their confidence.

Chapter 7

More on the Beginning: How It All Began

"Trust in the Lord with all your heart, and lean not on your own understanding"
Proverbs 3:5-6

It was December 15, 1990, and my career at Booz Allen came to an abrupt change one morning when John came into my office (the very nice one with a view of an arboretum) and announced that I no longer had a job. In one moment, after 13 1/2 years, I went from big-shot Vice President, head of the London office, partner in charge of our transport practice in Europe, to unemployed. They don't use the term in polite white collar circles, but I was "fired." I remember that numb feeling as I grabbed a taxi and headed for the train ride home. This was not a convenient time to be unemployed. My wife and I have two lovely daughters who were just getting ready for University. We were living in another country (England), owned a house with a mortgage, and I wasn't even sure if we would be allowed to stay in the country and work. It was a long, numb ride home. As always, Judy was a great encourager, but I was more than a little concerned. Booz Allen offered to pay our family's expenses to move back to the States. While that made sense in many ways, God was birthing a different plan in my heart — a plan that would bring many changes.

So, what does a consultant to industry do when his big-shot firm tells him to take a walk? Well, start his own firm of course! So, literally within weeks, WR Steinmetz & Associates was born. There were no "associates," and there were no clients; but I did have a nifty letterhead. So I used it and sent out over one hundred letters to former clients and contacts announcing the "glad" news of my new firm and my interest in working for them. Then I waited, and I waited, and I waited. Nothing came back for several months, and while no income came in, the expenses of living in expensive Surrey, England, kept coming in. Then, I got that nudge from God; and very quickly, I had a Romania connection — see Chapter 1.

I had a Romania connection but no income. I went in faith with Ronnie and learned a great deal, but I came back to no income and no prospects. My overactive, overachiever life and workstyle was going to be severely challenged. I remember visiting Guilford near our home in Surrey one weekday with Judy, wandering along High Street, looking in shop windows, gazing at the street vendors, and feeling completely lost. This was not my world. There was no deadline, no pressure, no competition. It was clear that what I had learned to lean on for significance was no longer there. I would learn that faith in God had to come first and then that acting through and in obedience to that faith was of the greatest significance. For it is in serving the Most High that we get the only true, real significance. Serving through the church and helping Romanians would teach me that and help me to teach others.

Then I got a call. The call was from Ross Sayers, a former client and chairman of the State Railway Authority in New South Wales, Australia. He had a project for me and wanted to know if I was available. I tried to not sound too desperate with my "yes." In a matter of several days, another colleague and I were in Sydney to begin the project. The project concerned train system control at the busy central stations in downtown Sydney. Visibility of trains arriving was almost zero, and mistakes were routinely made in prioritizing trains to tracks and platforms. A new central control system was desperately needed, and I could certainly design the functional specification for this system. But first, there was a challenge.

The unions were not convinced that this management consulting Yank from Britain could understand this real world railway problem, much less solve it. So, a meeting was set up with the various union leaders and me. The challenge was quite simple: How well do you know ... really know ... railway operations? I began going through my resume of railways from New York to London to San Francisco to Hong Kong. After about 15 minutes of this "riveting" monologue, they stopped me, certified me as qualified, and agreed that we could work together to solve their problem, which we did. One key output of the project was a massive flowchart that showed how all the key pieces of information needed to flow. They loved our work; they implemented it; and to my knowledge, no trains were subsequently "lost." Mission accomplished!

Chapter 8

The Lord Blessed With the Railway Technology Strategy Center (RTSC) *and* Our Love for the Romanian People Deepened

"Look at the birds of the air,
they neither sow nor reap or put away in barns,
and yet your heavenly Father feeds them."
Matthew 6:26

During that time, I accepted the role as an Assistant Pastor/Elder at a local Penta-Baptist church, Esher Green Baptist Church. My role included small group leading, occasionally preaching, treasurer, and coordinating our mission work. This latter work started with Romania and grew to include support for work in France, Hungary, and Ireland. The depth of this work varied greatly, but my principal passion remained the orphanages and churches in Roman, Romania. As described in Chapters 3 to 6, we made several trips a year to Roman and the surrounding area, at first with trucks, to bring much needed materials. Later, when more could be purchased in the area, we flew in to Bucharest Airport, Otopeni. During the early years of flying in, we would be picked up in Pastor Mugur's car (Pastor of the Roman AG church), a Dacia. This was always a harrowing adventure, and on one occasion, the car died. Eventually, we helped purchase a van; and Pastor Mugur became our go-to driver and coordinator in Roman. Costin was also our most trusted translator and led the worship at his church. There wasn't much that he couldn't do, and he always did everything well. Needless to say, these mission trips to Romania and elsewhere became an important part of our church. At one point, 60 of our 200 members made at least one trip to Romania.

All of this required resources – both the church's as well as our own personal resources. Esher Green Baptist Church remained very generous over the years, and much of this work was paid for out of both general giving and specific gifts through the church. On the personal level, I had a challenge. My independent consulting company had started very slowly, and it became apparent that many of my clients were buying the big name (i.e., Booz Allen & Hamilton) rather than just me and my abilities in the past. This was clearly another lesson in humility.

During that time, I had some really challenging projects. One was a World Bank review of the Polish State Railways (PKP) by another consulting company that hired me to be their on-site project manager in Warsaw. I quickly learned that "project manager" meant do everything, and the project proved to be a real nightmare. During the same period, I helped the same company do a review of the British Government's plan to reorganize British Rail. Our recommendations were rejected by the UK Government, leading to a strange horizontal fracturing of railway functions and decades of poor performance by the railway. Conclusions are obvious that railways are not the airline industry and should not be structured in the same manner. Nevertheless, the Government had their own consultants, and they wanted to do something big. So they split the railways horizontally into a railway infrastructure company (Railtrack), railway rolling stock companies, operating companies, and regulators — lots and lots of regulators. They ignored our recommendation through our work for British Rail to create integrated geographic operators that could compete against one another for this complicated airline model. The Government's decision, while it led to years of poor railway performance, did open up several major opportunities for my new consulting company.

During my years with Booz Allen, my principal client had been London Underground — the metro railway of London. My client was Tony Ridley, the Managing Director of the railway, and in later years, Leslie Lawrence, Tony's Engineering Director. During eight years of my time with Booz Allen, these two leaders provided projects that kept me and my staff busy and effective. Those projects were the foundation of my practice in London and helped me become a Booz Allen partner in 1987. I will always be thankful for the work that we did together from 1982 to 1989. But all things go through transitions, and in October 1987, a terrible fire occurred at the Kings Cross Station on the London Underground. The old wooden escalators caught on fire, and over 30 people died that terrible evening. The Government inquiry that followed found that the cleaning of grease, fluff, and debris under that escalator had been ignored for some time. When someone dropped a cigarette on a wooden escalator, a fire fanned by the wind from passing trains led to a tragic fire. The inquiry found several people responsible, including the functional manager and the finance staff who managed him. The functions we worked with had always improved productivity. The escalator maintenance function had been pressured into not fully cleaning under the escalators. This was a painful lesson that led to the dismissal of my principal client, Tony Ridley. So contracts with London Underground stopped, and with them, my partnership in Booz Allen also ceased. But what seemed like a disaster would turn into another blessing from God.

Several years into my private consulting company experience, Tony Ridley got in touch with me again. He was about to be appointed Professor of Civil Engineering at Imperial College, University of London. He wanted to know if I would join him in some function, yet to be defined. I said, "yes," of course I would. Then, another door opened. The directors of British Rail were being ordered to reorganize along the airlines model described earlier. Within this reorganization, they wanted to start a new research center, and Imperial College had been selected. Through a series of meetings, the question was asked: Would I consider being the Director of the new Railway Technology Strategy Center at Imperial College? It turned out that I could do this work as a contractor and charge consulting rates. I would be able to employ research associates through the University to support me, and they provided an office for the team to work from. It was the best of all consulting worlds, and it worked really well for years. But this model would get even better.

Every consulting practice needs a foundation client, one client that year after year will provide income and a reliable source of projects. In the past, with Booz Allen, that had been London Underground. This new research center had British Rail as its foundation client in its early years, but they were about to be disbanded. What company could take their place as our foundation client? The answer would come through an established technique I had used as a consultant in my earliest projects, reaching back to Philadelphia's SEPTA in 1976, New York's MTA in 1977, and San Francisco's BART in 1980. The technique was benchmarking, and its application was about to open doors I could never have imagined. The idea was originally called "The Group of Five." The metro railways of Berlin, Hong Kong, London, New York, and Paris thought that a benchmarking consortium could benefit them all. For this work, they would need a central resource; and why not a virtuous university and its "virtuous" Railway Technology Strategy Center? So within a few short years, we had a benchmarking consortium that grew to twelve metros and a second consortium of smaller metros that grew to fifteen clients. We did benchmarking and case studies for these 27 metros and employed consultant and research associates to this groundbreaking work. Everyone seemed to benefit and not the least myself. We stayed in the London area, continued as Assistant Pastors, and travelled routinely to Romania. God is so good! By the end of 1999, I was sensing that God was leading me to a deeper involvement in Romania and perhaps the biggest change in my life.

CHAPTER 9

A Call to a Greater Commitment

"The LORD God is my strength;
He will make my feet like deer's feet,
and He will make me walk on my high hills."
Habakkuk 3:19

Our trips to Romania had continued in the 1990's as I worked for different metro railways around the world. My diaries from that era make my head spin today. For example: The week of November 1, 1987, began in Singapore, then three days of meetings in London, followed by business meetings in London, Paris, and Marbella, Spain, the following week.

The prompting from God was simple: Why not move to Roman, Romania, and work with the churches and orphanage kids full time? They seemed to need us and want us, and the church we loved in England and the research center at the University increasingly needed us less. The decision came into focus one day while I was on a train going into London. It was a hot summer day, and the District Line trains were acting up again with long delays for travelers on trains that were not air conditioned. Why air condition London trains as it is only hot 30 or so days per year? On that summer morning, air conditioning would have been very appreciated. I looked around and saw young people, all at least 20 years younger than I was, sweating away with me. God showed me that day that it was time for a change, and a change indeed!

If we were to move, we had a house to sell, seemingly endless possessions (to sell, give away, and ship), a ministry at Esher Green Baptist Church, and a career to handoff to others. But in less than five months, it was all done. A good price for our home in East Horsley, Surrey, helped fund the endeavor; and in January 2000, we started the next phase of this adventure called "Serving Jesus." We packed to the brim our now aging BMW 735i and set off via Channel Tunnel car train to Paris. There, I attended my last benchmarking meeting with the growing number of metro railway representatives. When that was over, we said goodbye to my cousin Jocelyn and her husband and headed east. We knew the route well, having driven it numerous times in 7 ½-ton trucks over the previous nine years. This was different, as it was much more comfortable in our BMW; and it had a greater sense of significance, as we were going for long-term, full-time ministry.

The trip itself was both scenic and memorable. We stopped in a small town in Germany after a full day of driving from Paris. I don't remember the name of the town now, but I do remember how picturesque it was and what a fine dinner we had there; and the thought that maybe we should be tourists there for a day or two occurred to me. As it turned out, it would have been much easier and safer if we had just stayed another night.

Picture a full-sized sedan packed to the brim with all kinds of homemaking items. Judy is a wonder at many things, and she complements me perfectly as she loves details. Me ... not so much. Anyway, the BMW was packed to the brim with all kinds of items, which was fine at other borders, as we were just passing through. But at the border entering Romania, outside Oradea, again, it would be different. "Are you bringing in anything that you will leave in Romania?" the border customs agent asked us.

"Well, yes," we replied, "everything in the vehicle, including the two of us and the vehicle." He looked gravely at us, and we looked back at him, a little panic stricken – I am sure. Just the thought of unloading, much less reloading everything in that car, plus any duty to be paid, was horrifying.

The customs agent looked into the rear seat area that was packed to the brim. "What is that?" he asked. He pointed to a couple of Monet prints we had just purchased in Paris. We showed him. He was quite happy with that and said that we could proceed without further delay. He must have been an art critic. Seriously, that was one big miracle. But we would need another one very shortly....

We passed promptly through Oradea and entered the hill country leading to the Transylvania Mountains. Then, it started to snow. Now those of you who live in warmer climates, like Florida, are likely shivering at the thought of driving through a snowstorm over the mountains. If you are from the north country like we are ... well, we just decided to press on. There was only one issue. There were no, I mean NO, snowplows operating on Romania roads in 2000. But we decided to press on, following in a big tractor trailer's tracks. Only problem was, he pulled off the road after a while, leaving us to plow along through the snow. At one point, we tried to put chains on our vehicle, but that was just too difficult. So we pressed on – up the mountains. The good news was that we had a big, heavy BMW pushing the snow out of our way. The bad news was that we had a big, heavy BMW with an automatic transmission that liked to overrev when we went down grades. So Judy operated the handbrake, while I put it in neutral at each downgrade and gingerly drove onward mile after mile in the dark. Judy remembers several harrowing hairpins, including one that we got stuck on and had to power our way out of. I guess I have chosen to forget that part. Judy is sure to this day that an angel pushed us around that hairpin turn.

Our destination was a mountain town named Cluj-Napoca. We had been offered accommodation there by a wonderful lady who used to direct the nursing home in Roman — our ultimate destination on this odyssey. By another miracle, we made it safely to Cluj. But then our next problem appeared ... How do you find an address in a city late at night when you don't know the language very well? Solution ... find a taxi, show the driver the written address, and follow him. It worked, and the kind lady we had come to call "Doctor Director" kindly provided us with a hot meal and a warm bed for the night. The next day, the temperatures had risen; so our way forward was clear; and we arrived in Roman to a warm reception and an introduction to the apartment we had purchased. Our friends had painted the apartment walls and set up our furniture that we had sent ahead of us in a container from England.

CHAPTER 10

Settling in to Roman *and* Those Wonderful, Orphan Teenagers

"Pure and undefiled religion before God and the Father is this: to visit orphans and widows in their trouble, and to keep oneself unspotted from the world."
James 1:27

Judy is definitely a pioneering wife, and she took great pleasure in organizing our two-bedroom apartment. The unit overlooked a small park next to the town hall, and the kitchen window had a fine view of it all. So overall, we were quite happy with our new adventure. But inevitably, there were challenges.

Language was certainly one of them. We had several, able translators for preaching and business discussions. While Judy made endless amounts of brownies for our orphan teenagers, I was the shopper. This was a great way to expand my Romanian vocabulary. I started out with a lot of "here" and "there" in Romanian and a lot of pointing. It was clear that my lack of fluency was amusing to some of the shop clerks from their smirks. I guess I was the village idiot in many ways. I did get some respect though. One day when a clerk made an open joke about my hat, I responded in Romania, "Would you like it better with a feather in it?" She was embarrassed, and I enjoyed my small victory.

We had a series of outreaches during this time period, and many people would come and hear about how to have a personal relationship with Jesus, if for no other reason than that Americans were a novelty in Roman. But we weren't appreciated by all; at one meeting, some concrete was thrown at me. It didn't really hurt, and it provided me with an opportunity to be a good example of being peaceful to our young listeners. That particular meeting was in the park near our apartment, and one of the young people climbed a tree above us to get a better vantage. That inspired us to tell the story of Jesus and Zacchaeus to an appreciative audience.

My principal activity while in Roman was to start a micro-enterprise non-profit. The idea was to train those who wanted to start small businesses in various business disciplines, help them to prepare a business plan, and provide interest-free loans for the best plans. While I was sure that was what I could contribute locally, God had a bigger plan than I could have imagined. Sure, I could encourage the local pastors in Roman. But plant new churches? I would have declined that calling if God had put it in front of me; instead, He sort of snuck that part of this adventure up on me, one church at a time starting with an Assembly of God church in Roman. But first things first, there was this wedding....

During our years of visiting Romania, one of our most important resources was a young man named Costin. Cos was my translator, musician, counsel, and friend during this time. Over time, I felt genuine affection for him and consider him the son I never had. Well, as usually happens, Cos met a young lady named Alina. She is a bright "morning star" of a person and the perfect match for Cos. One night, we entertained them while they were still dating, with the movie *Titanic*. After the movie ended, Cos went home, and Alina slept in our extra bedroom.

Earlier, I mentioned challenges in those days; and one was the heating systems in Romanian apartment buildings. At that time, each town had a huge heating plant that piped hot water to all the buildings. Often in the winter, there would be too much heat; and then everyone would open their windows to let some of the heat out and some cool air in. Hey, who needs thermostats? But with this system comes the concept of a heating season — fixed dates in the calendar when the heat goes on and turns off. Well, it happened that on that night of the *Titanic* movie showing, the heat had been turned off for the entire town. It was officially spring. But someone had forgotten to tell the weatherman. It was still cold outside, and a concrete building without heat gets cold and clammy. So, not only was the apartment cold and clammy but so were the sheets. As I tried to warm up the sheets, I tried to be funny by repeating Leonardo's final words as he slipped under the water: "Rose, Rose!" Well, we started giggling and then wondering what Alina was thinking in the next room. We found out the next day as we drove her back to Suceava for her classes. Cos and Alina were whispering lightheartedly in the back seat. When Judy and I shared the full story, we all had a good laugh.

We returned in the spring and prepared for the big event — Cos and Alina's wedding. In Romanian tradition, the groom invites someone to be the wedding's godfather — sort of a best man, but a bit more. The "bit more" became apparent when the friends of the groom "kidnapped" the bride at the reception. I was required to drive around Roman with Cos looking for Alina and her kidnappers. Cos played it real cool and told me to just pretend to search. The bride was eventually returned to the reception, but I was taken to be a pretty poor godfather for not "rescuing her." The food was also different from our traditions with "sarmale," a featured food — grape leaves rolled around meat and rice. The cake was also different as it was soaked in a sugar syrup and covered with whipped cream. One other different aspect of the wedding was that the legal part had to be performed at the Town Hall, with the bride and groom dressed in business attire, before the church wedding with the bride in the traditional white gown and veil took place. The first legal wedding part was a holdover from the communist state days where the government took precedence over the church, and clergy had no legal right to marry couples. We learned that communist traditions and outlooks die hard.

The mayor of the Town of Roman was a rotund ex-communist who always seemed to regard me with a level of suspicion. Later on, I learned that he suspected I was a CIA agent spying on his government. Pretty amusing, but not so surprising as the communist mind believes in spying on everyone and that everything is the government's business. Perhaps because of these suspicions and wanting to keep a close eye on us, "His Honor" offered us a large meeting room for our business training sessions.

It was fun to educate these ex-communists in the virtues of capitalism and the more mundane disciplines of accounting. Some very good business plans were produced by these budding entrepreneurs, including a real estate company, a fish farm, a mushroom farm, a honey farm, and a pet shop. We funded most of these examples with interest-free loans, to varying levels of success.

Sadly, the pet shop lady decided to travel to the west to earn more money for the business start-up and died in a car accident while traveling through Hungary. There were a lot of sad stories from this era, and we quickly realized we could only try to help. Real help comes from God and Him alone.

During this same time framework, we helped Pastor Mugur start an Assembly of God church in Roman. Financial help came from several groups in the States, and before long, we had purchased an incomplete residence near the outdoor market and made plans for its completion. A construction team from a southern US state came to build an upper room on the top of this residence. I met this team while they were working on the top floor, and they complimented me on my English. When we cleared up the confusion, I did note that my southern drawl needed some work. When the building was completed, we decided to have an American Thanksgiving dinner as an outreach. While a good number of visitors came for the free food, some of the church people were not happy with gypsy families who came and left a real mess. Cultural interfaces are always difficult, even or especially in church life. The next day was Sunday, and we looked forward to visitors returning for a church service. But the weather turned unseasonably cold overnight, and a considerable snowstorm with high winds met us on Sunday morning. Needless to say, attendance was meager, and I wonder from this and other experiences how much influence Satan has over the weather.

     We grew very close to Costin's family, including his mother, Valerica. We have many fond memories of this time, including hearing horse carts coming down the streets early in the morning – a nostalgic sound that transported our thoughts to a simpler time when people couldn't rush around, but rather spent more time with people. Valerica's hospitality was exceptional, and her smorgasbord breakfasts were always a feast. Her parents, Cos' grandparents, were two of the finest people I met in Romania. They were one of those older couples that had been together so many years that they just blended together — like "bookends," as Paul Simon wrote. Grandfather had been forced to fight for the Nazi's and had been badly wounded during a winter battle. He said that if it hadn't been for the freezing cold, he would have bled to death. He survived that, and subsequently, many years in a Siberian prison camp. When released, he walked home, from Siberia to Roman, Romania. You figure out the miles, but it was epic, to be reunited with his wife and family. Love like that is worth a long walk.

Overall, our time in Roman was productive — helping the church grow, preaching on most Sundays, and complementing the church work with our micro-enterprise efforts. During that time, we also helped a church get organized in Toleti. The founders of the church were very grateful and gave us many of their woodworking items. We keep and treasure some of these items to this day. As we got more involved in Roman, we often found ourselves in a sort of tug-of-war between different families in the church and other churches. We realized that we were good catalysts for change but also that we could get in the way of a church maturing. Not surprisingly, God was opening another door for us in a nearby city.

CHAPTER 11

Bacau Beckons ... Then Fades to Another Call

"To everything there is a season, a time for every purpose under heaven"
Ecclesiastes 3:1

We first met Pastor Marian at a church meeting. We were instantly in love with this man of God and his vision for planting churches in the City of Bacau, which was located about an hour south of Roman. We started splitting our time between Roman and Bacau, often doing a morning service in one city and an evening service in the other. While our orphan teens were moving on to college and jobs, the church in Bacau was attracting young families and teens; and we were pleased to be used in this growing fellowship.

The drive home from Bacau was frequently made in the dark, and strange things were often seen along that lonely road, including packs of dogs running wild. One dark night, one ran out in front of our vehicle, and we hit it. I then did something I would never do elsewhere; I kept driving. I guess the packs of wild dogs had me intimidated.

On the way out of Bacau, there was a long, straight stretch of road that had a 25 mph speed limit for over a mile. One night, I got pulled over for doing 35 in the 25 mph zone. The officer recognized me as an American and asked me if he could give me a fine. Imagine that ... He asked me! I said, "sure, as long as I could get a receipt." I asked for a receipt, because in the communist era, these ticket fines were actually bribes that the police pocketed. He smiled and happily gave me a ticket. On another drive outside Bacau, we got waved over by a policeman on the side of the road. He indicated that our car had been weaving a bit while approaching him. In my simple Romanian, I said, "Socitia meo, spune ca... ." Before I could even finish, he cut off my explanation that my wife had been directing me and just waved me on with a smile. Obviously, he was a married man!

Pastor Marian was fun to work with but a bit breathtaking at times. Once, when stuck in traffic while driving in Bacau, he just drove his Dacia up on the sidewalk to avoid the traffic jam. It wouldn't have been that bad, but a lady pushing a baby buggy had to dodge us on the sidewalk. On another occasion, we were driving back from visiting Pastor Marian G. in Onesti, another church plant we were helping with, when our lights picked up a large cow in our lane. It was too late to brake, so Pastor Marian adroitly swerved to the left, only to face an oncoming Mercedes. I remember lifting my knees up to try to keep my legs from being crushed as we collided. And collide, we did! I was in the front seat; and Judy, Estera (Marian's wife), and their two children were in the back. We were all shaken, but basically, we were okay. We got out to inspect the car, and we were shocked to see that our Volkswagen was barely dented, but the full-size Mercedes was crushed in like an aluminum beer can. A head-on collision at high speed and only one car was severely damaged. Obviously, urgent prayer works as we had just defied physics, $Ft=mv$ for you physics majors.

Later on, I recalled the story that many damaged vehicles were sent from Germany to Romania and rebuilt. If the frames of these vehicles were bent, the Romanian mechanics would simply heat them with torches and bend them back. It looked like it worked, but of course, the heating process took most of the strength from a vehicle's structure. Is this what happened on that lonely road that night, or was it the prayer?

Either way, we were safe, healthy, and happy. All except for Pastor Marian and the kidding he took when he explained it had been a "really black cow." Really black!

It was a pleasure to help build up both the church and its building. I remember giving a gift of $300 to Marian and instantly rushing out to buy a new door for the unfinished building we had bought. He was right about the need, but the speed with which we could spend the money was breathtaking at times. We offered a seminar on micro-enterprise in Bacau during this era and were pleased to have the press attend. The resulting coverage was full of cynicism: "A scent of proselytism" was the headline with a full-page picture of me. Proselytism was a criticism the established church hung on any protestant, particularly one who was evangelizing. So, I assume I should have been honored with their intended insult, and after all, it was a pretty good picture.

During this time, we sold our apartment in Roman to Pastor Mugur and bought an apartment overlooking a park in Bacau. Our friends moved our household goods while we were at Christmas break with family, and we looked forward to returning later that winter to living and working in the much bigger city of Bacau. But God had other plans....

Chapter 12

A Call to Humble Service (Granville AG) *and* an Unfinished Story

*"Even the sparrow has found a home,
and the swallow a nest for herself"*
Psalm 84:3

    While we were home in Vermont for Christmas break, we learned that the pastor of the church we had been attending was moving on and that church, Granville Assembly of God (Granville, NY), was looking for a new Senior Pastor. Now, during this four-year period of our lives, we had become more involved with the Assemblies of God (AG), in part as we helped plant four new AG churches while in Romania and in part as our home church in Granville was an AG Church. But I was still taking some courses, and I was a long way from being credentialed by the AG. AG rules require applicants to be credentialed and live in the district the church is in, neither of which requirement did we meet. Nevertheless, there was that nudge again.

    From the Romanian perspective, the church planting era was mostly over; and we greatly believed that local pastors should lead the church, not foreigners/missionaries, no matter how gifted. From the Granville side, this little church had had two pastors for only five years each in its recent history. By the way, that was the minimum time a new pastor promised to stay with his church. So clearly, the need for stability and maturity was clear in Granville; the priority for national pastors to take the lead was also clear in Romania. So, unqualified as we were but with a clear nudge from the Lord, we applied for the position of Senior Pastor in Granville.

Apparently, we were second in line, but when the other candidate withdrew, we were asked to be candidates. We were amazed, and I thank the Superintendent of the New York District at the time who listened to our references and trusted in his Holy Spirit nudge. Thanks also to our references, especially Pastor Pat. So, after an interview with the search committee, we were asked to preach "with a view" on a Sunday in June; that was to be followed by a meeting with all the members. I remember saying that any candidate will say that he will love you all, but as we have been attending here part time for over 12 years, we can say that right now we already love you. We were voted in and began our ministry in Granville the first Sunday in July 2003. That was the easy part. The hard part was having to say a goodbye to the folks we loved in Roman and Bacau.

We did say our goodbyes, and through subsequent visits with members of our new church, we made it clear that our love and commitment would continue. There was a little understandable grumbling from some in Bacau as they had worked long and hard to set up our new apartment there. But God has a wonderful way of providing, as one of those families got to stay in our apartment rent free for several years. God always has wonderful ways of blessing us if we just stay faithful and honest.

Epilogue

John Sees the Light on the RTSC *and* a Sweet Reunion at the Airport: Confirmation of Both Our Coming and Our Going

"Delight yourself also in the Lord, and He shall give you the desires of your heart. Commit your way to the Lord, trust also in Him, and he shall bring it to pass. He shall bring forth your righteousness as the light, and your justice as the noonday."
Psalm 37:4-6

Since returning to America, we have returned to Europe many times for social purposes. On one of those visits, I searched out my old office at the University of London in South Kensington, London. I was curious to see if the Railway Technology Strategy Center still existed and, if so, what it was up to. I found a door with the RTSC name on it, knocked on it, and introduced myself to several research associates who were working away. They were so pleased to meet me, as I had been one of the initiators of this research group. They still had our old reports on the shelves, and they were still doing benchmarking and case studies as we had originally done them some 20 years earlier. Their boss, Richard, was not in at that time; but on the way out of the building, I came across my old nemesis, John, in the foyer and said, "hello." To my surprise, he greeted me enthusiastically and said how well the RTSC was doing. Further, he said that the RTSC had become a model for other university/industry partnerships throughout the University of London. More than that, the RTSC had been used as a showpiece in the university's recent application for funding to the UK Government, and it had worked really well. John had a real "Road to Damascus" experience, at least in regard to the RTSC. By the way, on a subsequent visit to London, I met with Richard, who turned out to be one of my former graduate students. He took Judy and me through an album of RTSC events, and there was a photo of President Xi of China, perhaps the second most powerful man in the world, sitting in front of an RTSC presentation booth. Not bad, but even more encouraging would be what happened on one of our return trips to Romania.

On this trip, Pastor Marian was to meet us at the Bucharest Airport. Before we saw him, we saw two other beaming faces, Costel and Alina P. Costel had been the oldest member of his family who was ushered into the orphanage, as his dad had killed his mother. He had said at one Bible study that there was no justice. We could hardly disagree with that observation from an earthly perspective. But he had given his heart to Jesus at one of those youth meetings and was now a University of Bucharest graduate with a good job. Just as encouraging was Alina P.'s story. Alina was an orphan kid in Roman the whole time that had we worked there. She had these big, sad, brown eyes and would ask us every time we saw her if we would please adopt her. We truly wanted to, but as we explained many times, we felt we had adopted all of the children already; and to select just one to legally adopt might have interfered with our larger "adoption" program. Well, Alina P. was finishing her PhD at the University of Bucharest and looking forward to a significant career and a productive life. We couldn't have been more encouraged.

Now, if you've gotten to this point in my story, you may be asking yourself: "Is this really 'The Greatest Adventure of All'?" And the point is that for me, it really is, because it is my story ... my story of walking with Jesus. Your story should be "The Greatest Adventure of All" to you. If it isn't yet, don't worry ... just ask Jesus for a nudge in the ribs. Then prepare to be part of your great adventure; and allow God to use your life in amazing and infinite ways!

"Therefore, I urge you, brothers and sisters, in view of God's mercy, to offer your bodies as a living sacrifice, holy and pleasing to God—this is your true and proper worship. Do not conform to the pattern of this world, but be transformed by the renewing of your mind. Then you will be able to test and approve what God's will is — his good, pleasing and perfect will."

Romans 12:1-2

"Old Reliable"

Our old BMW served us well in England for 15 years, in Romania when we lived there for four years, and afterwards when we visited with teams from Granville. One of our Romanian teens asked if he could have the vehicle when we were finished with it. Kevin C. was quick to point out there would be little left when we were done with it. When the power steering went on the way down a mountain years later, I realized we were, indeed, finished with it.

Journey Through the Snowstorm to New Ministry in Roman

Our Youth Group in Roman

Flying via Romanian Airlines (Air Tarom)

The early days of flying to Romania was via Air Tarom as they were the cheapest airline. They flew Russian Tupolev jets with very simple seats. We learned to pray a lot during these flights, and Psalm 46 was always a favorite — "We will not fear, though the earth give way."

Judy with Friend, Ramona

Brother Dwayne with Orphanage Kids

Micro-enterprise Efforts

Starting small businesses in an ex-communist country with a very weak economy was certainly a challenge. We made interest-free loans to many entrepreneurs with mixed results. One man said he was starting a fish farm on a rented property but always had bad luck. We later learned he was mostly a con artist.

Pastor Ray at Roman Family Dinner

Older Children at the Orphanage

Ana M.

One of our favorite people in Romania was Ana M. She translated for us many times and was our administrator for micro-enterprise in Bacau for a season. We attended Ana and Liviu's wedding during a later trip to Bacau, along with several brothers from our Granville church. We later visited them and their three very energetic boys at their home outside of Paris.

Orphanage Children with Soulful Looks

Alina P. with Pastor Bill

Success in Micro-enterprise

Some small businesses did take off, including a honey farm. The owner thanked us later on by giving us an enormous jar of honey, which we took back to the United States and enjoyed for many months. Is honey a processed food? We just walked straight through customs in Boston with the honey in tow.

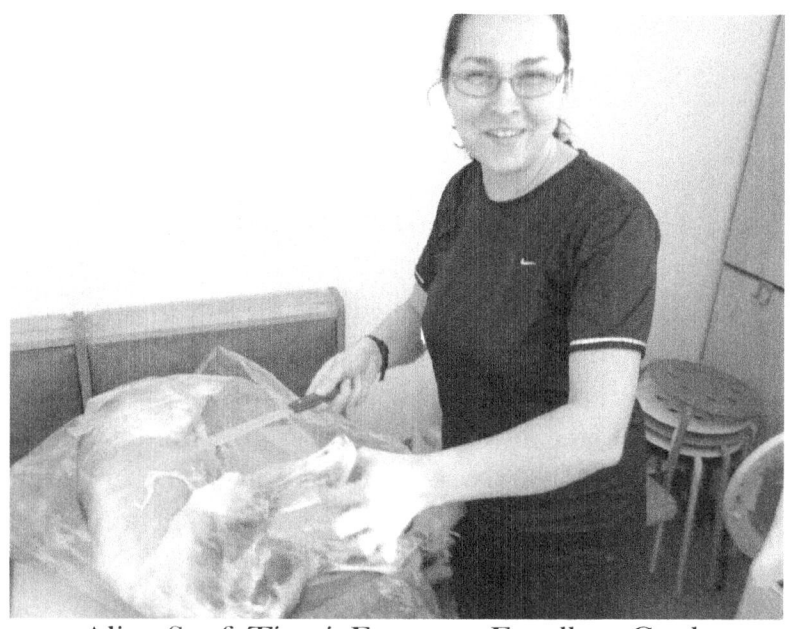

Alina S. of *Titanic* Fame, an Excellent Cook

Great Grandma and Fourth Generation Sami

Driving in Romania

The Romanians were quiet, peace-loving folks when in normal circumstances. But when many of them got behind a steering wheel, a transformation took place. One of the worst incidents happened on their major Route 2 that was being rebuilt at a very high standard. We were stopped for the construction when a vehicle passed us on the right at high speed. The problem was that the road dropped down a full five or six feet on the right side, and down he went. He seemed surprised as we drove by. His car was probably totaled by that indiscretion.

Ioan's Resting Place and His Grieving Family

Family Dinner at Cos' Home

Pentecostal Church Culture

One tradition in Pentecostal churches was the tradition of a prophet. While Biblically valid, the office in Romania was sometimes held by rather strange folks who would come late to a service, shout out something over the worship and prayer, and then quickly leave. On one occasion, one of these "prophets" declared that there were "foreign devils in our midst." We were the only foreigners present. I asked the pastor to set the record straight with the people, which he sort of did. But these so-called "prophets" had a great deal of influence.

Cos Translates for Me One More Time

Roman AG Church and The Next Generation

Micro-enterprise Help

My partner in all the micro-enterprise efforts was Kevin C. He was a generous, kind, and insightful participant. On one occasion, we went jogging together in Roman. Along with the danger from overexcited, stray dogs, we made a strange sight of two middle-aged men huffing and puffing around the streets of Roman, as jogging was rare there. Kevin was bigger than me, a bit slower too, and it sure looked like he was chasing me. Fortunately, the local police did not investigate.

Pastor Mugur with Members of Roman AG

Roman Baptist Church After Renovation

Prayer Warrior

One older man, who we met in Suceava, had been arrested numerous times for praying in public. His hands had been broken by the Securitate (secret police) many times, but he kept praying publicly. The Christian teens in his town would avoid him on the street, as he would instantly want them to kneel on the sidewalk and pray with him. His crown in Heaven must be magnificent.

Pastor Marian "Bacau AG" and His Son, Abel

My Mom Joined Us for One Trip and Loved the Children

Bors Soup

Not the Russian beet soup ... The Romanian bors soup is a meat and vegetable soup with a soured grain additive. A sour soup that was never my favorite, especially on a hot day, but had to be consumed with gusto to please our hosts. We always did just that!

Costel, Pastor Bill, and Friend

In Closing

May God bless and strengthen you, lead and guide you, and give you revelation concerning the great adventure that He has planned for your life, from this day forward.

SALVATION PRAYER

If you don't already know Jesus as your Lord and Savior and you want to, please pray the following prayer from your heart to enter into a relationship with Him:

Dear Jesus,
I admit that I'm a sinner, and I need You. Thank you for dying on the cross in my place and taking my punishment. Please forgive me for my sins, and come into my heart and be my Savior and my Lord. Please help me to live for You from this day forward. Thank you for making me part of Your family. In Jesus' Name, Amen.

If you prayed this prayer sincerely from your heart, you are now a child of God. You have just taken your first step in your journey with Him. Welcome to His family!

Your Great Adventure Awaits You!

Made in the USA
Middletown, DE
08 April 2023